KARATE KATAS
OF WADORYU

Shingo Ohgami

Dedication
To Hironori Ohtsuka, the founder of Wadoryu
and my Sensei

Published by Japanska Magasinet, Göteborg
Box 5231, 402 24 Göteborg, Sweden
Tel. 031-35 85 01

ISBN 91 9702 31-08

Cover and illustrations by Jan Carlsson
Photography by Bruno Edberg

Printed in Sweden by Typoprint, Göteborg

PREFACE

Wadoryu karate was founded by Sensei Hironori Ohtsuka (1892–1982) and it has become one of the most popularly trained karate styles in the world. But, unfortunately, the number of books written about Wadoryu karate is very few.

I have trained karate at Tokyo University Karate Club, one of the oldest Wadoryu clubs in Japan, under Sensei Hironori Ohtsuka. Since 1969, when I came to Sweden as a guest researcher in chemistry at Chalmers Technical University, I have been teaching karate in Gothenburg, Sweden. In the meantime I have written an introductory book of karate in Swedish. Fortunately, the book has received more applaud than it deserves and I have been asked occasionally to write a book of Wadoryu katas. I know that I am not the most proper person to do this job, but still I dare to because writing a book is a very good study for myself at the same time. As most of the Scandinavians understand English quite well and besides I still feel easier with English than with Swedish, I have decided to write this book in English. In this way even other English speaking people than Scandinavians could use this book for the training and studying of karate.

Personally I like to study katas even from other styles. It is fun to compare the difference in different styles. I hope that even other stylists can study Wadoryu karate and compare with their own.

What is most characteristic of Wadoryu?

Wa=peace, harmony, do=way, method, ryu=style, indicates a soft style. The katas trained in Wadoryu are also trained in other styles such as Shorinryu, Shitoryu and Shotokan. The difference in performance is rather small, but quite significant to characterize the style.

Wadoryu katas put more weight on the training of basic body movements of traditional budo arts. In Wadoryu katas you will find more similar movements to Kendo, Aikido, Jodo and other Japanese martial arts. They are: avoiding, escaping, entering, pushing, floating, etc.

The movements in Wadoryu katas are generally smaller than those in other styles. Whether it is good for the beginners or not, unnecessary movements should not be performed in Wadoryu katas. The movements should be performed by the shortest possible way. When the movements are smaller, it is more difficult to accelerate and focus. You need more skill to perform them effectively. In budo it has always been said that it is very important to learn from the old masters, since older people do not have the energy to do unnecessary movements. They perform techniques with the minimum necessary energy. Old masters perform techniques very rationally. Katas in Wadoryu are like that.

It follows that it will be more difficult to describe Wadoryu katas in such a form as a book. Anyway, I have used plenty of pictures and tried my best to explain especially for Western-, non-Japanese readers. If my way of explaining Wadoryu karate katas causes any kind of misunderstanding, I shall be the only one to be entirely responsible for it.

I would like to thank Mr. Bruno Edberg, who has taken the pictures, Mr. Jan Carlsson who has done the illustrations in this book, and Mr. Göran Svensson who is the model for some of the pictures.

Shingo Ohgami

About the author

Shingo Ohgami was born in Japan in 1941. He started training karate in 1960 when he entered Tokyo University (Todai) where Sensei Hironori Ohtsuka was the instructor of the karate club.

His interest in karate overwhelmed the idea of becoming a medical doctor so that he changed his major to chemistry.

He worked for a company as a chemical researcher between 1965 and 1969, where he also instructed karate. In 1969 he came to Sweden as a guest researcher at Chalmers Technical University in Gothenburg. Shortly after arriving in Sweden, he started a karate club. The club grew to such a proportion that he decided to give up a career in chemistry and has been engaged in teaching karate fulltime since 1972.

He was graded to 5th dan black belt by Sensei Ohtsuka in 1974.

Other than karate his interest spreads to Iaido (Japanese sword art, 5th dan Musoshinden-ryu), Jodo (Shintomusoryu), Aikido, Ryukyu Kobudo (Bo, Sai, Tonfa,etc.), Taichi Chuan (Chinese soft system), Ton Loon Chuan (Chinese Praying Mantis Boxing),etc. He is a member of the Japanese Budo Academy.

NOTES

o The main pictures are taken from the front and placed on the upper part of the pages.
o Side views, back views and applications are presented in smaller sizes and placed on the lower part of the pages.
o Once you understand the principle of a movement, you can find an uncountable number of applications. This book can show only a few examples,either a direct application or an indirect application.
o Some basic theories are introduced, which may help you to understand karate katas better.

CONTENTS

KATAS

KATAS IN KARATE

Kata is a composition of basic and advanced techniques of various kinds. Different kinds of stances, postures, hand techniques, foot techniques 'and body movements are composed into a completion. Karate is unique because of the existence of kata. Kata is a splendid invention as a media to inherit the art of karate.

As kata is an expression of a will, the number of katas and the way of performing kata is various. But still it is generally accepted nowadays that the katas trained in Okinawa can be classified into the following three:

Shurite	(trained in Shuri area)
Nahate	(trained in Naha area)
Tomarite	(trained in Tomari area)

Roughly speaking Nahate is a powerful and heavy karate. Shurite and Tomarite are light and quick.

Some of the katas inherited can be assorted as follows:

Shurite

Pinan (Heian)	Shodan, Nidan, Sandan, Yondan, Godan
Naifanchi (Tekki)	Shodan, Nidan, Sandan
Passai (Bassai)	Dai, Sho
Kushanku (Kanku)	Dai, Sho, Shihokushanku
Jitte, Jiin, Jion	
Gojushiho	Dai, Sho

Nahate

Sanchin	
Tensho	
Gekisai	Daiichi, Daini
Saifa	
Seisan	
Seipai	
Sanseiru	
Shisochin	
Kururunfa	
Seienchin	
Suparinpei	

Tomarite

Chinto (Gankaku)	
Rohai (Meikyo)	Shodan, Nidan, Sandan
Wanshu (Enpi)	
Wankan (Matsukaze)	

Others

Niseishi (Nijushiho)
Sochin
Ananku
Unsu
Seishan (Hangetsu)

The above mentioned katas have some variations. For example, Passai Kata has not only Dai and Sho, but also Matsumura no Passai (Passai of Matsumura), Tomari no Passai and Ishimine no Passai with some differences in performance.

Uechiryu karate has a different series of katas (Sanchin, Kanshiwa, Seishan, Seirui, Konchin, etc.), but a character of Uechiryu is Nahate type.

WADORYU KARATE

Wadoryu karate was founded by Sensei Hironori Ohtsuka.
Sensei Ohtsuka was born in 1892 and started training jujutsu already when he was 6 years old. He continued his study of jujutsu even during his stay at Waseda University in Tokyo. He received the license of Shindo Yoshinryu Jujutsu in 1921 from Tatsusaburo Nakayama. Around this time the Okinawan method of karate was introduced in Tokyo. He started training karate in 1922 with the famous Gichin Funakoshi. He has studied karate even with Kenwa Mabuni and Choki Motobu.
In short, Wadoryu karate is a compound of jujutsu and Shurite type karate. He has rearranged the following nine katas so that the students can study the principle of karate and Japanese old martial arts.

Pinan	Shodan, Nidan, Sandan, Yondan, Godan
Naifanchi	
Kushanku	
Seishan	
Chinto	

In this book I would like to explain about these nine katas.

The principle of avoiding, escaping, entering, pushing, floating etc.,can be seen in the arts of Kendo, Aikido, Jodo, Iaido,etc.
These katas are also trained in Shitoryu, Shotokan and Shorinryu, but you will easily find the differences which are so significant to characterize styles.

I try to outline Wadoryu katas as follows in technical development.

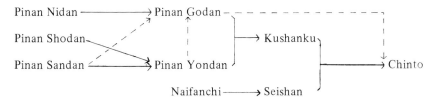

Pinan katas are summarized into Kushanku kata. Together with the completely other series Naifanchi- Seishan, Kushanku develops further to Chinto kata.

POSTURES

The postures of the body can be classified into the following three:

Mashomen (front viewing)
> The whole front part of the body faces the opponent.

Hanmi (half front viewing or half side viewing)
> The body faces the opponent at the angel of about 45°.

Mahanmi (side viewing)
> Only the side of the body faces the opponent.

The posture can be varied successively inbetween. The three mentioned above are the basic concepts.

STANCES

There are many basic stances in karate. Here will be mentioned Zenkutsudachi (front stance) and Nekoashidachi (cat stance) which are important to perform Pinan katas of Wadoryu.

Zenkutsudachi (front stance)

We define the stances in which the front knee is bent and the rear knee not. (zen = front, kutsu=bent, dachi=stance) The stances vary depending on what kind of techniques are performed.

Junzukidachi (junzuki stance)
> used to perform Junzuki (front hand punch) or other front hand techniques, see page 28 about the detail of Junzuki

Gyakuzukidachi (gyakuzuki stance)
> used to perform Gyakuzuki (reverse hand punch) or other reverse hand techniques, the stance will be slightly shorter but wider than Junzukidachi

Junzukitsukkomidachi
> used to perform Junzukitsukkomi (deeper junzuki), this is to reach as far as possible having the minimum balance

Gyakuzukitsukkomidachi
> used to perform Gyakuzukitsukkomi (deeper gyakuzuki)

Nekoashi (cat stance)

When more weight is put on one leg than the other and a part of the latter foot is raised a little bit above the floor, the stances are called Nekoashi (cat stance) named after the similarity to a light-moving cat.

Nekoashi is classified mainly to the following four:

Mahanmi no Nekoashi (side viewing cat stance)
> posture is side viewing, the front foot is directed toward the opponent and the rear foot a little bit backward, about 60 % of the weight on the rear and 40 % on the front

Hanmi no Nekoashi (half front viewing cat stance)
> the front foot toward the front, the rear foot 30° toward the front, the body is twisted to about 45° against the opponent

Mashomen no Nekoashi (front viewing cat stance)
> the front foot toward the opponent, the rear foot about 30°, though the body faces the opponent

Gyakunekoashi (reverse cat stance)
> more weight is put on the front foot than on the rear

Mahanmi no Nekoashi (side viewing cat stance) is very similar to so-called **Kokutsudachi** (back stance, ko=back, kutsu=bent, dachi=stance).
But in this book the author would like to use the traditional Wado terminology, Mahanmi no Nekoashi. The readers from other styles can understand this as Kokutsudachi (back stance).

UCHIUKE (INSIDE BLOCK) AND SOTOUKE (OUTSIDE BLOCK)

For example, the first block of Pinan Shodan is a forearm block which is performed from the inside to the outside. Sensei Ohtsuka uses a term 'haraiuke' (harai= parry, uke=block) in his book. Some people call this block 'Uchiuke' (uchi=inside, uke=block) because the block comes **from the inside.** But other people call this block 'Sotouke' (soto=out, uke=block) because the block goes **to the outside.**
The second block of Pinan Shodan with the left arm comes from the outside of the body to the inside. Some people call this block Sotouke and the other Uchiuke. There are people who call both blocks Udeuke (ude=forearm, uke=block) because the block is performed by using the forearm.
In this book the author would like to use the terminology as follows:

> **Uchiuke =** the block which comes from the outside of the performer **to the inside**
> In such a way we can translate this word into inward block.
> **Sotouke=** the block which comes from the inside of the performer **to the outside**
> In such a way we can translate this word into outward block.

(uchi=in, soto=out, uke=block in Japanese)

Mahanmi no Nekoashi
(side viewing cat stance)

Mashomen no Nekoashi
(front viewing cat stance)

PINAN

Pinan has five katas, namely Shodan, Nidan, Sandan, Yondan (Yodan) and Godan. In some styles Pinan is called Heian (the same letters can be read differently in Japanese). Pinan Shodan means Pinan No. 1 followed by No.2 – No. 5. In some styles Shodan (No.1) is changed to Nidan (No.2) and v.v.

It is said that Pinan katas are made or rearranged from Chan-nan kata by the famous Yasutsune Itosu (1830–1914) in the beginning of this century. Pinan katas are not so old but widely trained as basic katas among Shurite stylists such as Wadoryu, Shitoryu, Shotokan and Shorinryu. Pinan katas are excellent to learn the basic idea of Shurite type karate.

Among the five Pinan katas, Pinan Nidan has the least number of techniques. Therefore, we generally start with Pinan Nidan and then Shodan, Sandan, Yondan and Godan. It does not matter so much whether you train first Shodan or Sandan, because they are two different series. After those three katas, the order should be Yondan and then Godan. Totally,Pinan katas are summarized into Kushanku kata. Kushanku is known to be one of the very old katas. Some say that Y. Itosu got the idea of Pinan katas from Kushanku kata.

At the author's dojo we teach Taikyoku katas before we start Pinan series. Taikyoku katas were made by the late Gichin Funakoshi(1868–1957). Taikyoku katas consist of only two or three different techniques and give beginners a very good basic training. For example, Taikyoku Shodan consists of Gedanbarai and Junzuki (Oizuki).

Anyway,the official Wadoryu kata starts with Pinan Nidan, though Pinan Shodan is shown first in this book.

Pinan should be pronounced pin-an.

PINAN SHODAN

Pinan Shodan is not an easy kata for beginners, because the techniques in Pinan Shodan are mainly based on "double moment" principle, which is something different for the beginners. In karate, especially in Shurite, the whole body should be used to accelerate the technique. Body twisting is one of the most important factors among the methods of how to use the body. In normal punches and other basic techniques the body is twisted in the same direction as the punch itself.

But in "double moment" the body is twisted in the other direction than the technique itself. This principle is often used in blocking, as in Pinan Shodan, but also used for attacking techniques such as Uraken (back fist), Shuto Sotomawashiuchi (knife-hand punch to the outside),etc.

Look at the figure, suppose you are looking at the performer from the top.

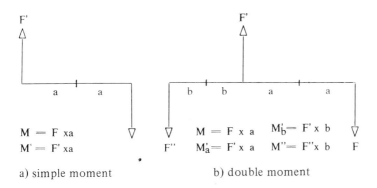

$$M = F \text{ xa}$$
$$M' = F' \text{ xa}$$

a) simple moment

$$M = F \text{ x a} \qquad M'_b = F' \text{ x b}$$
$$M'_a = F' \text{ x a} \qquad M'' = F'' \text{ x b}$$

b) double moment

In a) simple moment, moment M effects directly the moment M'. (In the case of punch, F' is left hand straight punch and F is your right hand drawing back to the side of your body.)

In b) double moment, M is first transferred to M'_a which together with M'_b effects in its turn M", in other words strengthen the effect of F". (In the case of No.1 of Pinan Shodan, F" is the left Sotouke, F' is the left side of your body, and F is the right side of your body.) The first movement of Pinan Shodan is left Sotouke. The body should be twisted slightly to your right while your Sotouke block goes toward the left. Compare later with the first movement of Pinan Sandan. The same Sotouke should be accelerated in a completely different way. The body is twisted to the left and the Sotouke block goes also to the left. These two different ways will be mixed in the coming Pinan Yondan.

On page 57 I have explained more about 'moment'.

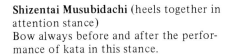

Shizentai Musubidachi (heels together in attention stance)
Bow always before and after the performance of kata in this stance.

Yoi (prepare)
Take Shizen Hontai (normal natural stance). Open your left foot a half step to the left and your right foot to the right and have Shizen Hontai. Your body should be kept in the same place. Make knuckles in front of your thighs at the same time..
'Yoi' means to 'prepare'. Prepare to start performing kata. Prepare for fighting. Be ready against your opponent from whichever direction he may come. This movement should be performed calmly, naturally and relaxed, but at the same time concentrated in mind.
This way of 'Yoi' is used in all the Pinan katas.

1. Step out with your left and take left Mahanmi no Nekoashi (side viewing cat stance).
Perform left Sotouke(outward block) Jodan. Bring your right hand to a protection form over your forehead. This is a training of Sotouke. So that your Sotouke will be effective, you have to twist your body to the right while your block goes to the left (double moment). By this body twisting, you can accelerate your block and avoid the opponent's attack. For this purpose the stance must be Mahanmi no Nekoashi in which you have your body in Mahanmi (side viewing stance). In Mahanmi no Nekoashi you should have your left foot toward your opponent and your right foot somewhat backward.

2. Stay in Mahanmi no Nekoashi. Perform left Uchiuke (inward block) Jodan and right Otoshiuke (downward block) Chudan.
This is a training to use both hands in different directions. Here left hand horizontally and right hand vertically. The application of this movement is very wide. Stay in Mahanmi no Nekoashi so that you can train the twisting of the body effectively without losing balance.

3. Draw back your left foot to have Shizen Hontai (normal natural stance).
Perform punch (Tettsui Yokouchi-sideward hammer punch, or straight punch) to the face.
This is a training to move back your front foot and perform a hand technique at the same time. The coordination of the body and hand is the key point.

4. Step out with your right foot and take right Mahanmi no Nekoashi. Perform right Sotouke Jodan and have protection form with your left. The body should be slightly twisted to the left. The same movement as in No.1.

application

5. The same as in No. 2.
Right Uchiuke Jodan.
Left Otoshiuke Chudan.

6. The same as in No. 3.
Draw back your right foot and perform
punch with your right.

application
For example block the opponent's punch
with your right and perform counterpunch with your left at the same time.

application
For example, you avoid the opponent's
sweep and perform counterpunch with
your right.

7–1. Intermediate
Bring your right hand down naturally after you have performed the former attack. At the same time twist the body to see what is happening on your back side.

7-2. Perform right Sotouke Jodan and right Maegeri (front kick) Chudan toward your right at the same time.
This is a training of performing hand technique and foot technique at the same time.
Application of this movement is wide. They can be: Jodanuke-Maegeri, Uraken-Sokuto, Tettsui-Sokutouke (side kick block),etc.

side view of No 7-2.

application

8–1. Intermediate
After the kick in No.7, draw back your right foot and prepare your hands for Shutouke (knife-hand block)

8-2. Step out with your left and take left Mahanmi no Nekoashi.
Perform Shutouke (knife-hand block) Jodan with your left. Shutouke is a good training for twisting the body in one direction and hand technique in the other (double moment). This Shutouke will be repeated 7 times in this Pinan Shodan.
Keep your left arm vertical to the floor so that you can use the maximum width of your arm for blocking. Twist your right arm in front of your solar plexus which will give your block a momentum effect and at the same time a protection of your body. ·

side view of No. 8-2.

9. Take one step forward with your right and have right Mahanmi no Nekoashi. Perform right Shutouke Jodan at the same time.

The body should be twisted 180° from the left side viewing stance to right side viewing stance. This is a very good training of co-ordination of body twisting and hand technique. The adequate body twisting also causes an avoidance from the opponent's attack.

Do not go up and down which is an abuse of the energy.

10. Take one step forward with your left and perform left Shutouke Jodan on left Mahanmi no Nekoashi.

application

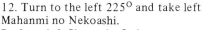

11. Take one step forward with your right and have right Junzukudachi (front stance). Perform right Tate Nukite (vertical spear-hand thrust) Chudan.

Perform your Nukite from where your right hand is (in front of the solar plexus). Do not draw it back to accelerate, otherwise the opponent would notice that you are coming.

12. Turn to the left 225° and take left Mahanmi no Nekoashi.
Perform left Shutouke Jodan.
This is a training of turning without losing balance. The principle of 'double moment' must be applied here, too. At the last moment your body must be twisted to the right while you perform your block toward the left.

side view of No 11.

13. Take one step forward with your right and have right Mahanmi no Nekoashi. Perform right Shutouke Jodan.

14. Turn to the right 90° and perform right Shutouke Jodan on right Mahanmi no Nekoashi. Here again the principle of 'double moment' should be applied.

15. One step forward with your left and take left Mahanmi no Nekoashi. Perform left Shutouke Jodan.

16. Move your left foot toward the left and have left Zenkutsudachi (Gyakuzuki stance). Perform right Sotouke Jodan at the same time.

This is a training of coordination between the body twisting (45° to the left) and hand technique toward the right. So on this stance you have to have your right side of the body a little bit ahead. (Gyakuzuki stance). Observe that Pinan Shodan consists mainly of this kind of opposite movement (double moment).

In the coming Kushanku kata this twisting of the body will be much deeper. (Kushanku No. 7 and No. 9, page 96, 97)

side view of No. 16.

17.1. Right Maegeri.   17-2. Left Gyakuzuki.

17. Perform Maegeri (front kick) Chudan with your right followed by left Gyakuzuki on Gyakuzuki stance.

side view   side view

18. On the same stance as in No. 17. Perform left Sotouke Jodan.
Bring your left hand down relaxed and twist your body to the right and perform Sotouke block toward the left at the same time (double moment).
The key to good focusing in such a small movement as this is a complete relaxation just before the performance.

19-1. Left Maegeri
19. Perform left Maegeri Chudan followed by right Gyakuzuki.

side view

side view

19-2. Right Gyakuzuki.

20. Take one step forward with your right and have right Zenkutsudachi (Junzuki stance).
Perform right Sotouke Jodan and bring your left arm to the front of your body which protects your front part and at the same time supports your right Uchiuke when it is necessary. The body should be twisted a little bit to the left while your right Sotouke goes to the right (double moment).

side view

side view

21. Turn to the left 225° on your right foot and have left Junzukidachi.
Perform Gedanbarai block with your left.
This is a training of coordination between the turning and sideward technique.
This technique will be repeated several times in Pinan Nidan.

22. One step forward with your right and have right Junzukidachi.
Perform Jodanuke (upward block) with your right
This is a training of coordination between the body movement and upward technique.
This technique will be repeated in Pinan Nidan.

When you perform Jodanuke or Gedanbarai, try to use the twisting of the blocking arm for acceleration. (Look at page 56, Energy equation.)

Use the twisting energy of your arm to accelerate your Gedanbarai.
Start your Gedanbarai by bringing your blocking arm in front of the opposite shoulder having your palm upward.
Complete your Gedanbarai by twisting your arm at the last moment.

Use the twisting energy of your arm to accelerate your Jodanuke. Start your Jodanuke as if you are performing a punch obliquely upward. Complete your Jodanuke by twisting your arm at the last moment.

23. Turn to the right 90° and have right Zenkutsudachi. (Junzukidachi). Perform Gedanbarai with your right.

24. One step forward with your left and perform Jodanuke with your left on Junzukidachi. The same movement as in No. 22.

application
Perform Gedanbarai and then counter attack.

Yame
Draw back your left foot naturally and have Shizen Hontai as in the beginning of this kata.
By 'Yame' you should come back to the same stance as you had in the beginning.

Naore
Bring your left foot to the center and then your right foot and have Shizentai Musubi-dachi (attention stance).
One should generally bow before and after the performance of kata with this stance. Yame and Naore should be performed exactly in the same way as this in all the Pinan katas.

JUNZUKI (OIZUKI)

For example, if you take one step forward with your right foot and perform a punch also with your right, this punch is called Junzuki or Oizuki. Junzuki is generally performed on Zenkutsudachi (front stance — see page 8), but it is also possible to have Junzuki on other stances.

Zenkutsudachi	—	Zenkutsudachi Junzuki
Nekoashi	—	Nekoashi Junzuki
Sanchindachi	—	Sanchin Junzuki
Shikoashi	—	Shikoashi Junzuki
etc.		

Here I would like to explain about Junzuki on Zenkutsudachi, which is one of the most important basic trainings. This Junzuki will be repeated in Pinan Nidan seven times.
The meaning of Junzuki is to reach an opponent who stands far from you.
But the more important meaning of Junzuki is to learn the coordination of body moving and punch (hand technique).
In Junzuki we have the following possibilities to accelerate the punch:

1. advancing (by stepping forward)
2. body twisting
3. arm stretching
4. arm twisting
5. weight shifting

Your Junzuki will be strong and effective when these elements are united (coordinated) into one.
If you succeed in coordinating with the full long step, you can coordinate even with a half step forward or a shorter distance of advancing. Junzuki will develop |further to Junzuki Tsukkomi (deeper Junzuki) and then Tobikomizuki which is a front hand punch with Suriashi (gliding).
Zenkutsudachi is important to train the shifting of the weight. At the last minute of the movement in Junzuki, the weight should be shifted from the rear leg to the front, which adds an enormous acceleration to the punch. The Chinese system, Taichi Chuan, gives a very good training of the weight shifting.

foot step of Junzuki

PINAN NIDAN

Trainees of Wadoryu karate generally start with this kata before Pinan Shodan. The number of techniques in this kata is fewer than Pinan Shodan and the movements in this kata are more fundamental. But it does not mean that this kata is less important. Some of the movements in this kata are advanced from the aspect of budo.
At the author's dojo in Sweden the beginners start with Taikyoku Shodan before they study Pinan Nidan. Taikyoku Shodan was made by Gichin Funakoshi and consists of Gedanbarai block and Junzuki (Oizuki).

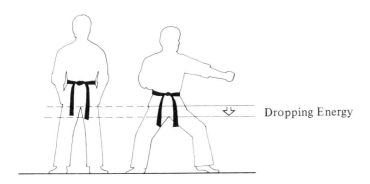

Dropping Energy

No. 1 of Pinan Nidan is a coordination of body dropping and downward technique.
Look at the energy equation on page 56. This is an example of using potential energy (mgh).

application of No. 1
Pinan Nidan

1. Step out with your left and have left
Mahanmi no Nekoashi (back stance, side
viewing cat stance).
Perform left Tettsui Otoshiuke (hammer
downward block).
This is a training of coordination between
body dropping and downward technique.
Downward technique (here Otoshiuke) should
be accelerated and given weight by the
dropping of the body. In order to learn this
coordination, the element of body twisting
should not be mixed. That is why the stance
used here must be Mahanmi no Nekoashi
which is a side viewing posture.
Application of this principle is wide. It can be
applied to all the downward techniques such
as Tettsuiuchi (hammer punch), Shutouchi
(knife-hand punch), Urakenuchi (back-fist
punch) and other downward blocks.
Practically, you can mix the effect of body
dropping with other acceleration such as
body twisting and weight shifting. But here,
in order to learn fundamentally the coordination between body dropping and downward
technique, we should purely make the down-

2. One step forward with your right and
perform right Junzuki.
In karate one should try to make the most of
the situation. Here you have the possibility
to twist the body from side viewing posture
to Junzuki which is about 120°. You should
use this twisting of the body to accelerate
your punch.

ward movement. (See page 29.)
As a basic training, do not bend your elbow.
You are apt to rely on the power of your
arm, when it is bent, which hinders the
coordination of the body.

3. Turn to the right 180° and perform right Gedanbarai on Junzukidachi.

This is a training of coordination between turning and sideward technique (here Gedanbarai).

The sideward technique should be accelerated by the turning. The technique can be Tettsuiuchi (hammer punch), Shutouchi (knife-hand punch), etc.

Why do we turn to the right instead of the left? From Shizen Hontai (normal natural stance) you have had your opponent on your left. After your action No. 1 and No. 2 is over, suppose you come back to the Shizen Hontai and from there you have your opponent on your right. Then you turn to the right and perform Gedanbarai. But in kata we do it directly from No. 2 which gives you a good training of turning.

4. Draw your right foot a half step back and perform Tettsui Otoshiuke (hammer downward block) with right on the Migishizentai (right natural stance, the stance is also called Migihanmi).

This is a training of coordination between pulling back of the body, raising up of the body and downward technique. Contrary to the No. 1 of this kata, the body goes up and the technique goes down.

Try to synchronize.

As a basic body training, do not bend your elbow, which may hinder the training of coordination between the body and the technique.

5. Perform Junzuki with your left.

6. Turn 90° to the left on your right foot and perform left Gedanbarai on the left Junzuki stance.
Try to coordinate the turning and block, based on the same principle as No. 3, but at a different angel.

application of No. 4

7. Take one step forward and perform right Jodanuke (upward block) on Junzukudachi. This is a training of coordination between one step forward and Jodanuke block. If you can coordinate this, you can easily coordinate this block with one step backward, too.

8. One step forward with your left and perform left Jodanuke on left Junzukidachi.

application
Jodanuke and counter attack

9. One step forward with your right and perform right Jodanuke on right Junzukidachi.

10. Turn to the left 225° and perform left Gedanbarai on left Junzukidachi. Coordinate the turning with the block.

Yu Nu Chuan Shu
(fair lady works at shuttles)
of Tai Chi Chuan

11. Perform Junzuki with your right.

12. Turn to the right 90° and perform right Gedanbarai on right Junzukidachi.

Lou Hsih Au Pu
(brush knee and twist step)
of Tai Chi Chuan

13. Perform Junzuki with your left.

14. Turn to the left 45° and perform Gedanbarai on left Junzukidachi.
You will find it more difficult to coordinate the turning and block in a smaller angle of turning such as this one. The key to the success in coordination is a complete relaxation just before the performance of the technique.
Front view is the same as No. 6 of this kata (page 32).

application
Gedanbarai

15. Perform Junzuki with your right.   16. Perform Junzuki with your left.

side view   side view

Look at the foot steps on page 28.

17. Perform Junzuki with your right.

18-1. Intermediate
Turn to the left 225° on your right foot and have Mashomen no Nekoashi (front viewing cat stance). Have your left hand on your right to prepare Nukite (spear-hand thrust).

This is just an intermediate.
Do not stay in this stance.

side view

18-2. Step forward with your left and finish with Shikoashi stance.
Perform left Nukite at the same time. Twist your right hand in front of your solar plexus. The right hand protects your front part of the body and at the same time gives a momentum effect by twisting.

This is a very important movement from the aspect of budo. By twisting the body from front viewing Nekoashi (cat stance) to side viewing Shikoashi, you can avoid the opponent's attack. And at the same time by using the same energy which is used in avoiding, you can accelerate your counter attack (here it is Nukite).
(See page 42.)

19-1. Intermediate

19. Step forward with your right, passing Nekoashi as in No. 18-1, perform right Nukite by twisting the body into Shikoashi stance.

19-2.

20-1. Intermediate

20. Turn to the right 90° on your left foot, passing right Nekoashi, perform Nukite as in No. 19.

application

20–2

21-1. Intermediate
21. Step forward with your left and perform Nukite as in No. 18.

application

From fighting stance right attacks with Mawashigeri. Left glides in with body twisting and gives a counterpunch.

Yame
Draw back your left foot and have Shizen hontai in the same way as in Pinan Shodan.

21-2.

Four possibilities of Irimi (entering movement)

Pinan Nidan No. 18, 19, 20 and 21 are the basic training of entering movements. Practically, there are four different possibilities as shown in the pictures.

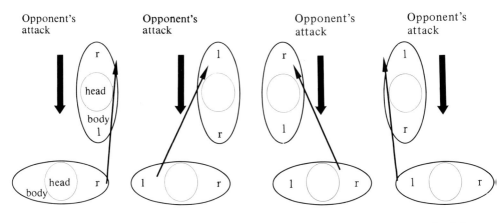

l = left
r = right

PINAN SANDAN

The techniques in Pinan Sandan are different from those in Pinan Shodan. Here in Pinan Sandan the techniques are mainly accelerated by body twisting in the same direction as the techniques themselves. Compare the Sotouke block in No 1. Pinan Shodan and No. 1 in Pinan Sandan. These are the two ways to accelerate Sotouke block. These two are mixed in Pinan Yondan which comes after Pinan Sandan.

These two ways of acceleration can be applied to other techniques than Sotouke. Gedanbarai block is applied principally in these two ways. Even Uchiwaza (circular hitting) such as Shutouchi (knife-hand hit), Urakenuchi (back-fist hit) and Tettsuiuchi (hammer-fist hit) must be accelerated in one of the two ways.

application of No. 8—10.

1. Turn to the left 90° and have left
Nekoashi (cat stance).
Perform left Sotouke Jodan.
This is a training of coordination between
the turning of the body and Sotouke
block which goes in the same direction.
In order to train the complete coordination between the two elements, the
stance here must be front viewing posture
– Mashomen no Nekoashi (front viewing
cat stance).
Compare carefully this movement and
Pinan Shodan No. 1. These two represent
the two ways to use Sotouke coordinated
with the body movement. (See page 43.)
The left hand should go to block as
directly as possible from the front of your
thigh. Unnecessary movements should not
be performed.

2. Take a half step forward with your
right and have Heisokudachi (closed toes
stance).
Perform right Sotouke Jodan and left Gedanbarai at the same time.
This is a training to use two hands in different ways at the same time.
Application of this movement is very
wide. It can be:
Uraken-Gedanbarai, Haitouchi-Gedanbarai,
Sotouke-Gedanuchi,etc.
Heisokudachi is an unstable stance. But
it is a good way to check the former
Nekoashi in which we should have our
front toe toward the front. That is why
the stance here is Heisokudachi (closed
toes stance).
side view on page 45

3. The same stance as in No. 2.
Perform right Gedanbarai and left
Sotouke at the same time.
Repeat the same movement as in No. 2.

4. Turn to the right 180° and have
Mashomen no Nekoashi (front viewing cat
stance).
Perform right Sotouke Jodan at the same
time.
This is based on the same principle as in
No. 1. Turning and Sotouke should be
coordinated. For that purpose it is
necessary to turn perfectly 180° into
Mashomen no Nekoashi.

side view No. 2   side view No. 3

5. Take a half step forward with your left and have Heisokudachi.
Perform left Sotouke Jodan and right Gedanbarai at the same time.
The same movement as in No. 3

6. The same stance as in No. 5.
Perform left Gedanbarai and right Sotouke Jodan at the same time.
The same movement as in No. 2.

applications of using two hands

a. right Gedanbarai
left Urakenuchi

b. left Sotouke
right Groin attack

c. left Sotouke
right Punch

7. Turn to the left 90° and perform left Sotouke Jodan on Nekoashi.
For the same reason as in No. 1 and No.4, the stance must be front viewing.
No. 1 of Pinan Sandan is the side view of this posture.

8. Take one step forward into right Junzukidachi.
Perform right Tate Nukite (vertical spear-hand thrust) Chudan.
Keep your body straight just as in basic Junzuki.

side view

9. Turn your body 180° to your left as if you are escaping from the opponent's grip.
This is a training to turn your body sharply.

10. Turn to the left 180° and take Shikoashi stance.
Perform left Yoko Tettsuiuchi (sideward hammer punch) Chudan.
From the previous position raise up your body sharply and perform counterattack with Tettsui.
In No. 9 someone has a hold on your right hand. You try to escape from him by pulling yourself back with the whole body. In No. 10 he is still holding you and pulling. So you follow his pulling and the last minute give him a counterattack. (See page 43.)
Application of this movement is wide. Instead of Tettsui you can make Uraken (back-fist), Shuto (knife-hand), Enpi (elbow), etc. Anyway, this is a training to escape from the seize of an opponent.

side views

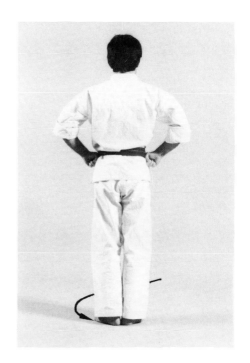

11. Perform right Junzuki.
After Tettsui in No. 10 you give the opponent a punch. Tettsui-Tsuki is a very common combination technique. In kata you step out to perform Junzuki. In practice it can be a punch on the same place as in No. 10.

12. Turn to the left by drawing your left foot to your right and have Shizentai Musubidachi (attention stance).
Bring your hands onto your hip to have a protection form. Have your elbows on the same line as your body so that the opponent cannot find the sides of your body.
This is a protection and preparation for the next block.

side view

side view

13–1 Koteuke.

13. Take one step forward with your right and have Shikoashi stance.
Perform right Koteuke (arm block) which is followed by Yoko Tettsuiuchi (sideward hammer punch) Chudan with the same hand. This is a training of Koteuke.

13–2 Tettsui Uchi.

It is necessary to coordinate the body twisting with the block so that the block will be strong enough. Koteuke is generally followed by Tettsui as here or Uraken (back-fist) Jodan.

side view

side view

13–3 Draw back your Tettsui and have protection form.

14–1 Koteuke.

14. Take one step forward with your left and perform left Koteuke-Tettsui on Shikoashi stance.
The same movement as in No. 13.

side view

side view

14–2 Tettsuiuchi.

14-3. Draw back your left hand and have a protection form.

side view

side view

15−1. Koteuke.

15−2. Tettsuiuchi,

15. Take one step forward with your right and perform Koteuke-Tettsui on Shiko-ashi stance.

In No. 13 and No. 14 the Tettsui hand was immediately drawn back to the hip in order to have a protection form. But here in No. 15 the hand is not drawn back, because this is a part of a combina- tion technique followed by the next movement (Junzuki). This combination is the same as No. 10 and No. 11 of this kata.

At the same time it is also possible to check if your Tettsui movement is done correctly.

application

16. Perform left Junzuki.
No. 15 and No. 16 is a combination technique.

17-1. Intermediate
Bring your right foot forward and pass Shizenhontai (normal natural stance).

side view

side view

17-2. Turn to the left 180° by moving your left foot and have Shizenhontai. Perform right punch backward over your left shoulder and left Enpi also backward. This is a training to use the twisting of the body on such a high stance as Shizenhontai. Be careful not to lose balance when you focus your movement.
As an application you can think of a situation where you are held from your backside. You drop your body down and perform a counterattack with punch and elbow punch.

18. Glide a little bit to the right and perform left punch backward over your right shoulder and right Enpi at the same time.
The same movement as in No. 17.

Yame
Twist back your body to the left and have Shizenhontai.

 →

application

STUDY ABOUT TSUKI (PUNCH)

Let us look at Tsuki (punch) from the point of dynamics. This discussion is important because one can apply it to other karate techniques such as different hand techniques, blocks and even kicks. An effective punch, that is to say, a destructive punch is a punch with high energetic possibility in the word of dynamics.

According to basic physics, the energy equation is:

$$E = mgh + 1/2\ mv^2 + 1/2\ m\ (r\omega)^2$$

Terminology   E= energy, m= mass, g= gravity acceleration (980 cm/sec^2)
h= height, v= velocity, rω= angle velocity

The equation means that dynamic energy is the sum of potential energy, kinetic energy and rotational energy. In order to get higher energy, as m and g is constant, it is possible:

1. to use the difference in height (h) − potential energy
2. to increase the velocity (v) − kinetic energy
3. to use the angle velocity (rω) − rotational energy

It is limited to use the difference in height as we have to think about other elements such as balance in body. Typical examples of this sort of acceleration are Sokuto-fumikomi (stamping kick downward) and Gedanzuki (punch downward) to an opponent whom you have thrown down.

And No. 1 of Pinan Nidan is a training to use potential energy (page 29).

Angle velocity can be used by twisting the arm during the punch. This is limited to 180 degrees, but you have to make the most of it.

The biggest possibility to gain energy is to increase the velocity. It is naturally understood that an effective punch is a fast punch.

Let us study further about velocity. For eaisier understanding, let us take a simple acceleration.

$$v = at \qquad a=\text{acceleration}, \qquad t= \text{time}$$

So is v a function of acceleration (a). Further

$$l = 1/2\ at^2 \qquad l= \text{length between the hand before the punch and target.}$$

So we can get the following equation:

$$v = \sqrt{2 \times l \times a}$$

This equation shows that the longer the distance between the hand and the target is, and ` the higher the acceleration is, the higher velocity you can gain. The possibility to have a longer length is limited, but this is the reason why we perform the basic punch from the side of the body (the longest possibility). And also we can say that we need a proper distance to perform the most powerful punch.

So we concentrate on the acceleration now.

$$F = ma \qquad m= \text{mass}, \qquad a= \text{acceleration} \qquad F= \text{force}$$

This equation shows that force is needed to gain acceleration. In the human body the force is produced by muscles. It is necessary that many powerful muscles should take part in the action coordinated in a correct way. If you have performed your punch only by your arm, it is not enough. The key to perform a faster punch is to use as many muscles

as possible. Especially the muscles around body and hip are strong and these must be used effectively.
One can think about three possibilities to use these muscles for the acceleration of the punch. That is:

1. waving of the body
2. twisting of the body
3. shifting of the weight of the body

The type 1. acceleration (waving of the body) can be seen in volleyball, tennis, badminton,etc.,when they smash in the ball. This is also possible in karate and must be taken into consideration. But as basic karate we have to think about the balance of the body before and after the performance of the technique, so we leave it here for a while.
The most used and important is the typ 2 acceleration (twisting of the body). You can accelerate the punch and you can still keep your balance by having correct stances. There is also the third possibility to accelerate the punch and it is weight shifting. One can gain an acceleration energy by shifting the weight from the rear leg to the front.

In Pinan Yondan No. 7 and No. 10 are Yokoenpi (sideward elbow strike) . It is necessary to twist the body very sharp as the length of this strike (1) is much shorter than a normal punch. In other words Enpi is a good training of the twisting of the body.

MOMENT
Let us look at the twisting of the body closer. Generally the ability to twist something around a point is expressed by 'moment'. In the figure they are:

$$F_1 \times a_1 \text{ and } F_2 \times a_2$$

Especially when F_1 and F_2 are parallel to each other, it is called a 'moment of a couple' and both F_1 and F_2 have the same effect to twist the bar (in this case of punch it is body). By pulling back the other hand you can get a momentum effect which helps to twist the body. And this twisting causes an acceleration for the punching hand.
Further, the effective element for moment is the vertical element to the axis ($F_1 \cos \theta$ in the figure) and

$$F_1 \cos \theta \leqslant F_1$$

$F_1 \cos \theta$ is maximum when θ is 0. That is to say the momentum effect will be maximum when the punch is performed 90° to the body line.
We should not leave our arm or elbow from this straight line, that would decrease the momentum effect. $\longrightarrow 90^\circ$ principle

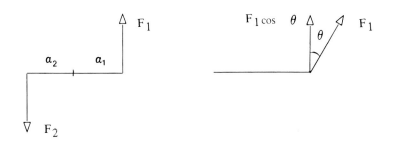

RELAXATION BEFORE AND AFTER THE MOTION

Every movement in our body is done by muscle contraction. A muscle contracts when it gets stimulation from the nervous system. If a muscle is tensed already in the original stage, it will be

tensed — relax — contraction

and this is two steps. If you are relaxed in the first stage, it will be

relax — contraction

and naturally this is quicker.

After the motion the muscle should immediately come back to relaxation and be ready for the next motion.

In many sports instructors tell their students to be relaxed. In karate this relaxation is very important. In the inside system of Chinese boxing they insist on this relaxation training very much (for example Tai'chi Chuan).

BACK SWING

Let us look at the figure on the right. This spring vibrates when it gets pulled on the bottom. Here a force is caused which wants to come back to the origin O, which is proportional to the distance from the origin O. Our muscles work in this way, too. So if you move the muscles in the opposite direction just before you perform some movement (for example, if you twist your body in the opposite direction before you perform punch), you will be given an extra acceleration. It can be compared to the back swing in golf. A disadvantage of this type of acceleration is that the opponent can recognize that you are going to do something, and that is not good. Therefore, this type of acceleration must be used carefully like in 'punch — punch' or 'block — punch' combination techniques.

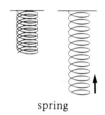

spring

KIME (FOCUSING)

When our punch meets the target, it gives a shock (energy) to the target and at the same time we get the same amount of shock back through our hand, arm and body (Law of action and reaction). Just at this very moment the muscle must be strained in order to receive the impact. Here is also a reason why we have to have a correct and balanced stance. The velocity of the punch starts from 0 and passing the maximum finishes with 0. In order to reach high velocity within the limited length, we have to accelerate the punch as quickly as possible. (Decelerate as quickly as possible,too). That is to say the velocity curve must be steep. It means that the movement must be sharp.

This state of straining and sharpness is called 'kime' (focusing) and is one of the important factors in karate. Karate is different from the Chinese system (especially inside system) which has a softer idea of kime.

Look at the energy curve on page 90.

PINAN YONDAN

No. 4 of the Pinan series is called Pinan Yondan or Yodan. Technically, Pinan Yondan is a summary of Pinan Shodan and Pinan Sandan, where two different types of acceleration – coordination of body twisting are mixed. No. 1, 2, 4, 17, 18, 19, 22 and 23 are Pinan Shodan type (double moment) and No. 7, 10, 13, 14, 15 and 16 are Pinan Sandan type (single moment).

Instead of Sotouke in Pinan Shodan, Haishuuke (overhand block) is included in this kata. Haishuuke is commonly used against Mawashigeri (round kick) Jodan or punch to the face. Shutouke of Pinan Shodan is replaced by Sotouke which will give you a basic training of Yakusoku Kumite of Wadoryu where Nagashiuke (nagashi= sweep away, clean away, uke=block) is mainly used.

All the Pinan katas are summarized into Kushanku kata. Especially this Pinan Yondan stands very close to Kushanku kata.

Principle of Nagashiuke

Generally speaking, when two forces collide with each other, the strength of the collision is strongest in (a) and then (b) and smallest in (c). The case (a) is generally used as a principle of attack so that the opponent receives the maximum shock. This principle is sometimes used even for blocking. The case (b) is a principle of basic blocking such as in Jodanuke, Gedanbarai, Uchiuke, Sotouke and Otoshiuke. In practice the idea of (b) develops further to principle (c) by which you can perform a block more effectively. Your blocking should work as if you are helping the opponent's attack. This movement is called 'Nagashi' (sweep away or clean away). If you perform a block by following this principle, then the block is called 'Nagashiuke'. If you combine this movement with a punch, then the punch is called 'Nagashizuki'. See page 86, No. 17 of Pinan Godan. (F= opponent's attack, f = your block).

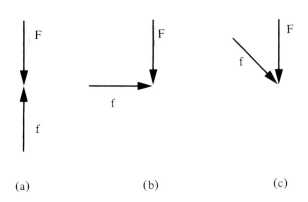

(a)   (b)   (c)

1. Step out with your left and have left Mahanmi no Nekoashi. Perform left Haishuuke (over-hand block) Jodan while your right hand is brought into a protection form over your forehead. Principally this technique should be performed according to the double moment. The left-hand block goes to the left and the body is twisted slightly to the right.

2. Bring back your left foot to the original position and then, step out with your right and have right Mahanmi no Nekoashi.
Perform right Haishuuke Jodan at the same time.
The same movement as in No. 1.

application

3−1. Intermediate

3. Bring back your right foot to the original position and step out with your left and have Junzukidachi.
Perform X-block with both hands from the sides of your body. It is difficult to use twisting of the body when you use both hands at the same time in this way. By relaxing completely just before the performance of the technique, you can

3−2

focus it better. The element of weight shifting must be applied here (page 57). When you use two hands at the same time, your face is completely open to your opponent. It is also necessary to relax immediately after the performance of a block in order to be ready for the next attack. Use twisting of the arms to accelerate your block.

application

4. Take one step forward with your right and have right Mahanmi no Nekoashi. Perform right Sotouke Jodan while your left hand forms a protection in front of your solar plexus.
This technique should be performed according to the double moment principle, the same movement as No. 1 and No. 4 of Pinan Shodan.

5. Bring your left foot forward and have Heisokudachi (closed toes stance).
Prepare your hands for the next movement. This technique could be a Kagizuki (hook punch) as an application.
Officially, this is a preparation.
Toes should be together because in Mahanmi no Nekoashi in the last movement the right foot was exactly directed to the front. As this is a preparation this should be performed calmly.

side view

6. Perform left Gedanbarai and left Maegeri to your left at the same time. This is a training to use hand technique and foot technique at the same time. Application of this principle is very wide; it can be Uraken–Sokuto, Sotouke–Kingeri ,etc.

7. Left Zenkutsudachi (here Gyakuzuki stance).
Perform right Yoko Enpi (sideward elbow punch) to your left hand as your imaginary opponent.
Enpi is a weapon to use against a near target. As the reach of your weapon is very short, it is inevitable to use twisting of the body. In other words, Enpi is a good training of twisting of the body. Keep your body straight and twist your body sharply. Look at page 57 about twisting of the body.

8. Bring your right foot to your left and have Heisokudachi.
The same as in No. 5.
As an application it can be Kagizuki (hook punch).

9. Perform right Gedanbarai and right Maegeri to your right at the same time.
The same movement as in No. 6.

application

11−1. Intermediate, preparation.

10. Left Enpi on right Gyakuzuki stance.
The same as in No. 7.

11. Turn your body to your left 90° and
have Gyakuzuki Tsukkomi stance (but
here the body is kept straight).

11-2.

Perform right Tenohirauke (palmar block) and have your left hand in protection form over your forehead.
The turning and the block should be coordinated so that the block is effective.

12—1. Right Maegeri Chudan.

12. Keep your hands as they are and perform right Maegeri, which is followed by Tate Uraken (vertical back-fist) on right Gyakunekoashi (reverse cat stance).

side view

application

12—2. Intermediate. Left hand is performing downward block.

During the Uraken the left hand performs a downward block and is drawn to the side of the body.

After the block in No. 11, you perform Maegeri and then move into the opponent and give him Uraken.

12-3. Right Tate Uraken Jodan.

This combination of simultaneous Uraken-Otoshiuke is very traditional. It can be seen in many of the Chinese systems such as Taichi Chuan, Tonlon Chuan, etc. In Matsumura no Passai this technique is repeated many times.

application

14−1. Right Maegeri

13. Turn to the left 225° on your right foot and have Nekoashi (cat stance). Perform left Sotouke Jodan.
This technique is the same as in No. 1 and No. 4 of Pinan Sandan. As this is a training of coordination between turning and blocking; you have to turn completely. The stance here must be front viewing cat stance (principle of single moment).

14. Perform a combination of right Maegeri, right Junzuki and left Gyaku-zuki.

back view

back view

14-2. Right Junzuki

The purpose of a combination training is to perform each basic technique as perfectly as possible even if it is a part of a long series. It is necessary to relax for a short while between each technique.

14-3. Left Gyakuzuki.

As the movement of the body is the most important, the stances should be Junzuki stance for Junzuki and Gyakuzuki stance for Gyakuzuki, which means a slight change in each punch. This should occur naturally by body twisting.

back view

back view

16—1. Left Maegeri

15. Turn to the right 90° and have right Nekoashi.
Perform right Sotouke Jodan.
The same movement as in No. 13, the stance must be Mashomen no Nekoashi (front viewing cat stance).

16. Perform a combination of left Maegeri, left Junzuki and right Gyakuzuki.
The same as in No. 14.

back view

back view

16-2 Left Junzuki.

16-3. Right Gyakuzuki.

back view

back view

17–1. Intermediate

17. Turn to the left 45° and have left Mahanmi no Nekoashi.

Perform left Sotouke Jodan and right Otoshiuke with your back fist.

This Sotouke should be performed

17–2

according to the double moment. (Twist your body to the right while the block goes to the left.)

This is also a training of using both hands at the same time.

back view

back view

18. Take one step forward with your right and have right Mahanmi no Nekoashi.
Perform right Sotouke Jodan and left Otoshiuke with back-fist.
The same movement as in No. 17.

19. Take one step forward with your left and have left Mahanmi no Nekoashi.
Perform left Sotouke Jodan and right Otoshiuke with back-fist.
The same movement as in No. 17 and No. 18.

application

side view

20. Twist your body to the left and have left Mashomen no Nekoashi.
Perform right Sotouke Jodan.
The main purpose of this movement is the change of the stance from side viewing Mahanmi no Nekoashi to front viewing Mashomen no Nekoashi, which means a sharp twist of the body of 90°. And this twist of 90° should be used to accelerate the block.

21. Perform right Hizageri (knee kick) and draw back your hands at the same time.
Draw your hands as if you are pulling your opponent. Try to keep your shoulders relaxed so that you can keep your balance during the kick.

back view

back view

22—1. Intermediate

22. Turn to the left 225° and have left Mahanmi no Nekoashi.
Perform left Kakeuke (hook block) Jodan and right Otoshiuke (downward block) with your palm Chudan.
This is a training to use both hands in different directions, one hand vertically and the other horizontally.

22—2

This type of combination of two blocks, Kakeuke and Otoshiuke, is seen in many katas, such as in Shisochin.
The body should be twisted to the right while your Kakeuke goes to the left (double moment).

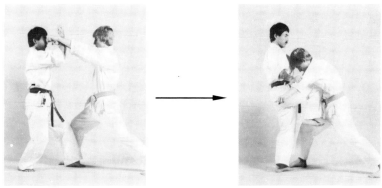

application of No. 20—21.

23. Turn to the right 90° and glide forward (suriashi), and have right Mahanmi no Nekoashi.
Perform right Kakeuke Jodan and left Otoshiuke with palm Chudan.
The same movement as in No. 22. When you glide forward, bring your right heel to the floor so that you can stamp on the opponent's front foot and then stand on your right toes.

Yame
Draw back your left foot and then right foot to have Shizen hontai.

application

application

PINAN GODAN

Pinan Godan will give you a little bit different impression from the other Pinan Katas. Pinan Godan seems to be inspired by Tomarite and will give a good preparation for the coming Chinto kata which is derived from Tomarite. Tomarite is known to be light-moving including jumping. Even Kushanku and Passai will be easier by training Pinan Godan as basic.
From the view point of Wadoryu, No. 17, No. 20 and No. 21 are unique. They are the techniques of avoiding and entering which are very essential to the traditional martial arts, budo.

No.12.

No.13.

No14.

side views

No.15.

No.16.

No.17

side views

1. Turn to the left 90° and have Nekoashi (cat stance).
Perform left Sotouke Jodan.
This is a training of coordination between turning and blocking in the same direction. The Nekoashi here must be Mashomen (front viewing) so that you can turn completely. The same movement as in No.1 Pinan Sandan.

2. Perform Chokuzuki (straight punch) with your right.
Nekoashi is a rather unstable stance. Draw back your left hand as sharply as possible so that the right punch will be strong enough.
No. 1 (block) and No. 2 (counterattack) is a combination technique.

application

3. Draw your right foot to your left foot and have Musubidachi (attention stance). Have your hands in preparation form. This is similar to No. 5 and No. 8 of Pinan Yondan, but we generally have it higher here, although lower than that of Naifanchi. As a preparation this should be performed slowly. As an application this can be Kagizuki (hook punch).

4. Turn to the right 90° and have right Nekoashi.
Perform right Sotouke Jodan.
The same movement as in No. 1, the stance must be front viewing.

application

5. Perform Chokuzuki with left.
The same as in No. 2.

6. Draw your left foot to your right and have Musubidachi.
The same movement as in No. 3.
This can be Kagizuki as an application.

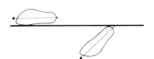

7. Take one step forward with your right and have right Mahanmi no Nekoashi. Perform right Sotouke Jodan. Have your left hand in protection form. This block is based on 'double moment' where the body is twisted to the left and the block goes to the right.

8. Take one step forward and have left Junzukidachi.
Perform Jujiuke (X-block) downward, from the sides of your body.
The same movement as No. 3 of Pinan Yodan.
Use the twisting of the arms to accelerate your block.

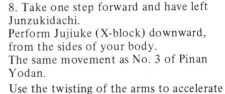

side view

9. Perform Jujiuke (X-block) upward with Shuto (knife-hand).
Perform the two blocks just as in the basic Jodanuke. Twist your arms as late as possible so that you can use the twisting energy of the arms for blocking.

10. Perform left Shotei Otoshiuke (palm-hand downward block) and right Haishu Otoshiuke (over-hand downward block) at the same time. No.8, No.9 and No. 10 are performed with the same stance with both hands at the same time which is relatively unusual in Shurite-type karate. But this combination can be seen later in Kushanku kata and Chinto kata.
Here in No. 10 the position of the two hands should be changed during the performance, which indicates a grip technique as an application.

applications

82 PINAN GODAN

(a)

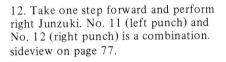

11. Perform left Chokuzuki (straight punch).
In order to make this punch strong, you have to draw back your right hand as sharply as possible so that the momentum power effect works.
This is also on the same stance as No. 8 — — No. 10. Body twisting in microscale is required to accelerate all of these techniques.

12. Take one step forward and perform right Junzuki. No. 11 (left punch) and No. 12 (right punch) is a combination. sideview on page 77.

(b)

(c)

13. Turn to the right 180° around your left foot and have Shikoashi stance.

Perform right Gedanbari.

Suppose your opponent comes from your front, you draw back your body and escape from his attack. Another opponent comes from your back with a kick, therefore you perform Gedanbarai at the last moment. Similar to No. 3 Pinan Nidan but this one has a different direction and stance. Try to carry the whole body as one unit so that you should not lose balance during the performance. This kind of turning will be repeated in Chinto kata and Passai kata.

side view on page 77.

14. Draw back your left foot a little and have Shizenhontai (normal natural stance).

Perform left Harai-Uchi (block-punch) Chudan.

The same movement as in No. 3 and No. 6 in Pinan Shodan. This is a training to move back your body and perform a hand technique at the same time. This block should go directly from your left side of the body so that you should avoid the unnecessary delay in time. It is why this block is performed like Uchiwaza (hitting) and it has the effect of both block and attack.

side view on page 77.

15. Take one step forward with your right and have right Zenkutsudachi (Junzukidachi). Perform right Yoko Enpi (sideward elbow punch) toward your left hand as your imaginary target. Keep your body straight and twist your body effectively. In some styles Mikazukigeri (crescent kick) is added before this Enpi, then it will be the same as in Passai kata.

side view on page 77.

16. Bring your left foot forward and have Gyakunekoashi (reverse cat stance). Perform right Sotouke Jodan and have your left hand in protection form. Suppose someone sweeps you from the rear and another opponent comes at you with a punch from the front; you take away your left foot quickly to avoid sweeping and perform Uchiuke to block your face.

As an application your left hand can be Osaeuke (press block) and your right hand can perform Uraken (back-fist attack).

In order for the next movement to be done perfectly, this stance must be front viewing.

sideview on page 77.

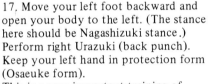

18—1. Intermediate.

17, Move your left foot backward and open your body to the left. (The stance here should be Nagashizuki stance.) Perform right Urazuki (back punch). Keep your left hand in protection form (Osaeuke form).

This is a very important training of Nagashi (sweep away, avoid).

By opening your body to the left, you can avoid the opponent's attack, and at the same time you can use the energy of opening (body twisting) for your counter-attack. The body must be twisted to the left as sharply as possible. This technique is commonly seen in Tonlon Chuan (Praying Mantis Boxing).

side view on page 77.

18. Jump and raise your feet up as high as possible. Turn to the left 270° and land on the toes.

Perform Jujiuke (X-block) downward as you land.

Suppose someone sweeps you with a Bo (stick weapon); you jump and raise your legs up to avoid the Bo. When you land, you protect yourself with Jujiuke.

application of No. 17.

18-2. Jujiuke

Choose the most difficult knee position on landing, which means the easiest to change your stance for the next opponent. Jumping is seen in Tomarite most often. Northern Shaolin has a lot of jumping techniques. In general, jumping is a risky technique. But training of jumping is very important in order to gain the lightness and sharpness of the body. As an application, you can perform Uraken or punch at the same time of jumping. Or, you can make a kick in the air.

19. Take one step to the right and have right Junzukudachi.
Perform right Sotouke Jodan and have your left hand in protection form.
The same movement as in No. 17 Pinan Shodan.

side view

20. Open your body to the left (Nagashizuki stance).
Perform right Sotouke Jodan and left Gedanbarai at the same time.
By bending the body backward, you can avoid the opponent's attack to your face.
Opening, bending and hand techniques must be coordinated into one unit.

21-1. Draw back your left foot to your right foot and have Musubidachi. This is a preparation.

side view

21–2. Move your right foot forward at an angle of 45° and have Nagashizuki stance. Perform left Sotouke Jodan and right Gedanbarai at the same time. As in No.20, the body twisting, bending backward and hand techniques should be coordinated. This will give you a kind of entering technique. The body should be twisted as if you are going into a narrow space. Bend your body as if you are avoiding the opponent's attack to your face. The twisting should occur in 21-2, not in 21-1. The hands in No. 20 and No. 21 are regarded as Kamae (preparation) in Wadoryu, though the movements are done sharply. This kind of entering method will be repeated in Chinto kata.

Look at page 206 for application.

Yame
Draw back your right foot and have Shizenhontai.

ENERGY CURVES

Karate is originally a system for fighting and therefore we have to refine our techniques so that they should have a maximum effect. We have to reach as high an energy level as possible at the moment when our attack reaches our opponent. Actually, we do not need any high energy level before or after this moment. In other words, all we have to do is to concentrate the energy at the very moment of contact. This energy concentration is called Kim (focusing) and is one of the most important factors of karate. (page 58)
Look at the figure 1). This shows an ideal energy curve of let us say a punch. This curve shows a minimum of energy until the very last moment and reaches the maximum at the moment of contact C). Masters' punches are like this. Total energy spent is shown by the ar under this curve. Masters can perform an effective punch by using a minimum of necessary energy. That is why old masters can perform an effective punch without being tired.
It may take the whole life before we can make a punch like this curve. As it is very difficult to follow this curve from the beginning, several methods of training have developed in the history of karate, which is a part of the reason why we have different styles.
In Wadoryu and also in Shitoryu the trainees are taught to follow this curve from the very beginning. They are always told to be relaxed before and after the performance of the techniques.
In Shotokan style it seems like they are taught to spend a longer period of high energy level as shown in figure 2) at least when they are beginners. They have proved that this method gives a very good result. That is why the Shotokan stylists look very powerful when they perform techniques.
In Gojuryu or in Nahate they have a famous training method such as Sanchin. It it a training of tension and the energy curve is like figure 3). This is also proved to be a very effective method to learn energy concentration.
In Taichi Chuan of the Chinese system they train techniques with the minimum of energy from the beginning to the end. Figure 4) shows the energy curve of Taichi Chuan. Taichi Chuan artists have shown that this is a very effective method for fighting.

I have explained 4 different methods of training from the viewpoint of energy concentration. It is impossible to say which method is the best. Some may prefer to follow one of the methods. Some may mix various methods in their program.

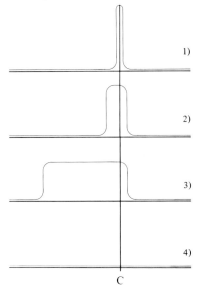

1)

2)

3)

C= contact the opponent

4)

C

KUSHANKU (KOSOKUN)

The name, Kushanku, is one of the oldest which can be traced in the record. It is said that a Chinese official called Kushanku came to Okinawa in 1762. Kushanku kata is probably a system which he has brought with him. Whether the story is true or not, you will find more similarity to the Chinese system, northern Shaolin, than other karate katas.
Kushanku is a kata of variety. It has a lot of various combinations, turnings, jumping and even creeping.
Most of the basic techniques in Kushanku kata have already been introduced in the five Pinan katas. It would be most proper to train Kushanku kata after you have learned all the Pinan katas.
Kushanku kata of Wadoryu is actually Kushanku Dai (dai=big). Other than this Kushanku there are Kushanku Sho (sho=small) and Shiho Kushanku (shiho=four directions).
Chibana no Kushanku (Kushanku of Chibana), Kuniyoshi no Kushanku and Chatanyara no Kushanku are also famous.
Gichin Funakoshi has changed the name of this kata to Kanku Dai (kan=observe, because of the first movement of this kata (making a circle with two hands).

Yoi (prepare)

Yoi of Kushanku is a little bit different from that of Pinan katas.
(Compare with the beginning of Pinan Shodan.)
Open first your left foot and then right foot and have a little bit wider Shizen Hontai (normal natural stance). Bring your left hand on your right hand at the same time.

1—1.

1. Make a circle with both hands slowly and calmly.

This is a way to show that you do not carry weapons. And more important, the circle symbolizes the universe. In order to be one with the universe, the circle should be made calmly, but concentrated in mind. It is as if you have a big ball in front. In Taichi Chuan (a Chinese soft style) the movements should always be circular.

1−2.

2. Step out with your left and have left
Mahanmi no Nekoashi.
Perform left Haishuuke (over-hand
block) Jodan.
The same stance as in Pinan Shodan,
Nidan and Yodan. Haishuuke is already
trained in Pinan Yodan No. 1 and No. 2
(double moment). Have your right hand
in protection form in front of your
body.

3. Bring back your left foot to the original position and then step out with your right to have right Mahanmi no Nekoashi. Perform right Haishuuke Jodan.

4. Bring back your right foot and have Shizen Hontai.
Have your left hand on your right as preparation (the same as in No. 5 and No. 8 of Pinan Yodan).

application of No. 2 and No. 3

5. Left Gedanbarai on the same stance (Shizen Hontai).

6. Right Chokuzuki (straight punch) Chudan on the same stance (Shizen Hontai). No. 5 (block) and No. 6 (counterattack) is a combination.

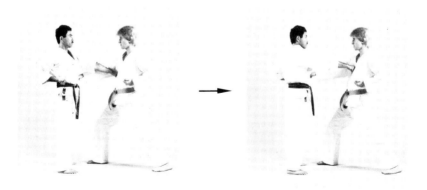

application

7. Step out with your left foot and have Gyakuzuki Tsukkomi stance.

Perform right Sotouke Jodan.

It is important to twist your body to the left adequately so that you can avoid the opponent's attack. This is a training of coordination between body twisting to the left and block to the right (double moment). The same block is trained in No. 16 of Pinan Shodan. Here is applied a deeper stance such as Gyakuzuki Tsukkomi stance.

8. Come back to the original Shizen Hontai.

Perform left Chokuzuki Chudan.

The energy of this coming back should be used to accelerate the punch. No. 7 (block) and No. 8 (counterattack) is a combination.

application

9. Step out with your right and have right
Gyakuzuki Tsukkomi stance.
Perform left Sotouke Jodan.
The same as in No. 7. Twist your body
adequately. No. 4 — No. 9 can be seen
also in Passai kata.

10. Bring your left foot to the right so
that the center of the body stays at the
same point.

10−2.

Perform right Sotouke Jodan and right Maegeri Chudan toward your right at the same time. The same movement as No. 7 of Pinan Shodan.

11. Draw back your right foot and then step out with your left and have left Mahanmi no Nekoashi.
Perform left Shutouke (knife-hand block) Jodan. The same movement as No. 8 of Pinan Shodan.

side view

side view

12. Take one step forward and have right
Mahanmi no Nekoashi.
Perform right Shutouke.

13. Take one step forward and have left
Mahanmi no Nekoashi.
Perform left Shutouke.

14. Take one step forward and have right Junzukidachi.
Perform right Tate Nukite (vertical spearhand) Chudan.

15. Turn 180° to the left and have left Gyakuzuki Tsukkomi stance.
Perform right Tenohirauke (palmar block). Left hand in protection form. The same movement as in Pinan Yodan No. 11.
Open your left foot adequately so that you can twist your body.
Look at No. 20 for a front view of this movement.

side view

16. Perform right Maegeri.
The same movement as in Pinan Yodan No. 12.

17. Turning your body to the left, drop your body down.
Perform left Gedanbarai and have your right hand in protection form. Suppose someone attacks you from behind. As soon as you notice it, you drop your body down as suddenly as possible to avoid it. So that you should be ready for the next movement, you should stand on your toes and the right foot should be directed toward the inside.

This movement is often seen in the Chinese system. The left foot can be used even for sweeping the opponent. Anyway, this is a very good training for a strong and soft knee.

side view

18. Perform Jujiuke Gedan (X-block). This is a sort of preparation for the next movement.

19. Stand up quickly by drawing back your left foot into Shizen Hontai. Perform left lower punch.
This is a training to perform a technique from such a difficult position like No. 18. The energy to stand up should be used to accelerate the punch. It is an application of No. 3 of Pinan Shodan. Strong leg muscles are required to perform it correctly.

application of No. 17
Avoid the opponent's attack by sinking your body.

side view

20. Turn to the left 90° by opening your left foot and have left Gyakuzuki Tsukkomi stance.
The same movement as No. 15 of this kata. Perform block with your right and protect your forehead with your left.

21. The same as No. 16.
Perform right Maegeri Chudan.

application of No. 17
Sweep backward.

application of No. 17
Sweep inward.

22. The same as No. 17.

23. The same as No. 18.

side view

side view

24. The same as No. 19.

25. Draw your left foot to your right and have Heisokudachi (closed toes stance). The same as Pinan Yondan No.5.

side view

back view

26. Perform left Gedanbarai and left Maegeri to your left at the same time. The same as Pinan Yodan No. 6 .

27. Have left Gyakuzuki stance. Perform right Yoko Enpi (sideward elbow punch). The same as Pinan Yodan No. 7.

back view

back view

28. Draw your right foot and have Heiso-kudachi. The same as Pinan Yodan No. 8.

29. Perform right Gedanbarai and right Maegeri to your right at the same time. The same as Pinan Yodan No. 9.

back view

back view

30. Left Yokoenpi on right Gyakuzuki stance. The same as Pinan Yodan No. 9

31. Turn to the left 180° and have left Mahanmi no Nekoashi.
Perform left Shutouke Jodan.

back view

32. Step out with your right 45° and
have right Mahanmi no Nekoashi.
Perform right Shutouke.

33. Turn 135° to the right and have
right Mahanmi no Nekoashi.
Perform right Shutouke.

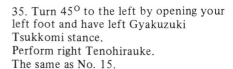

34. Step out with your left 45° and have left Mahanmi no Nekoashi.
Perform left Shutouke.

35. Turn 45° to the left by opening your left foot and have left Gyakuzuki Tsukkomi stance.
Perform right Tenohirauke.
The same as No. 15.

side view

36-1. Perform right Maegeri Chudan.

36-2. Step out with your right foot and have right Gyakunekoashi (reverse cat stance).
Perform right Uraken (back-fist) Jodan while your left hand performs Otoshiuke (downward block).
The same movement as Pinan Yodan No. 12.

side view

side view

37. Step back with your left and right, and have right Junzukidachi.
Perform right Sotouke Jodan.

38-1 Left Chokuzuki.
38. Perform left punch and then right (Renzuki).
Both punches must be accelerated by the body twisting.

side view

side view

38–2 Right Chokuzuki

39–1 Intermediate

39. Turn 180° to the left on your left foot.
Raise your knee (prepare for kicking), make Nukite (spear-hand) with your left and fist with your right (both prepare for hand attack).

side view

side view

39–2

Left hand hits the right knee and then right hand.

This is also one of the fine parts of Kushanku kata. Turn as suddenly as possible. By hitting with your left hand, you can make a surprise sound to distract the opponent. Stay for a while on your left leg to see what is going to happen next.

40. Drop your body and land on the floor with your right foot and two hands. Suppose an attack comes toward you. You drop your body as low as possible in order to avoid it. Keep your weight on your feet, not on your hands, so that you can be better prepared to stand up whenever necessary.

You can drop your body quicker if you relax in No.39-2. Relaxation between the movements is the key to advance.

side view

side view

41. Turn to the left 180° by raising your body and have left Mahanmi no Nekoashi.
Perform left Shutouke Jodan.
Strong leg muscles are required to be able to stand up quickly.

42. Take one step forward and have right Mahanmi no Nekoashi.
Perform right Shutouke Jodan.

side view

side view

43. Turn 270° to the left with Suriashi (gliding) and have Nekoashi.
Perform left Sotouke Jodan.
The same movement as Pinan Sandan No. 1. Turning and block should be synchronized in the same direction. The stance must be front viewing. Add Suriashi (gliding) to the turning, as if you are gliding into the opponent, which will give you a good training of balance.

44. Perform right Chokuzuki Chudan. The same as Pinan Godan No. 2.

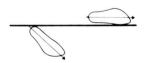

46-1 Left Chokuzuki

45. Turn 180° to the right with Suriashi (gliding) and have right Nekoashi. Perform right Sotouke Jodan. This is a training of coordination of turning, gliding and block. The stance must be front viewing.

46. Perform left and right Chokuzuki Chudan. Try to use the body for each punch.

application

46–2 Right Chokuzuki

47

47. Perform right Sotouke Jodan and right Maegeri to your right at the same time. The same as in Pinan Shodan No. 7.

side view

48. Draw back your right foot and then step out with your left and have left Mahanmi no Nekoashi. Perform left Shutouke.

49-1. Perform left Shotei Otoshiuke (palm-hand downward block). Drop your body down a little bit so that the downward block should be accelerated. Coordination of body dropping and downward technique is trained in Pinan Nidan No. 1.

application

50−1

49-2. Take one step forward with your right and have right Junzukidachi. Perform right Tate Nukite (vertical spearhand) while your left hand is kept in Osaeuke (press-block) form.

50. Turn 180° to the left and have Shiko-ashi stance.

side view

50—2

Perform left Yoko Tettsuiuchi (sideward hammer punch) Chudan. Suppose someone holds your right hand. Keep your right hand where it is and turn to the left. At the last minute you release yourself, from his seize.
This is an application of Pinan Sandan No. 9 and No. 10.

51. Suriashi (glide) forward in Shikoashi. Perform right Tate Uraken (vertical backfist).

side view

side view

52. Suriashi in and have left Gyakuzuki stance.
Perform right Yoko Enpi (sideward elbow punch). No.50, No. 51 and No. 52 in combination.

53. Open your body to the right and have Shizen Hontai.
Perform left Sotouke Jodan and right Gedanbari at the same time.
Use the energy of opening the body for acceleration of the blocks.

side view

side view

54. Turn 180° to the left on your right foot and have Shikoashi stance. Perform left Sukuiuke (scooping block) and right Sotouke Jodan at the same time. Turn sharply as if you are avoiding the opponent's attack and at the last minute perform the blocks. Turning must be used for acceleration. No. 53 and No. 54 in combination.

55. Perform right Sukuiuke. Sukuiuke is generally used against a front kick.
Look at page 128 for application of Sukuiuke.

side view

side view

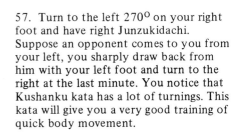

56. Perform Jujiuke (X-block) Jodan. The same as in Pinan Godan No. 9.

57. Turn to the left 270° on your right foot and have right Junzukidachi. Suppose an opponent comes to you from your left, you sharply draw back from him with your left foot and turn to the right at the last minute. You notice that Kushanku kata has a lot of turnings. This kata will give you a very good training of quick body movement.

side view

side view

59−1 Kick with left in the air.

59. Perform kicks in the air. Left and then right.

58. Perform Tettsui Otoshiuke (hammer downward block) with both hands. At the last minute of No. 57, you notice that your opponent comes to you at your body, so you perform blocks at this moment.

side view

side view

59-2. Kick with right in the air.

59-3. At the moment of landing, have right Junzukidachi.
Perform right Tate Uraken Jodan.

side view

side view

60−1

60. Turn 270° to the right.
Perform hand sweeping with both hands.
Do not bend your body. Bend your knees
instead so that you can make an effective
sweeping. In kata we train sweeping
with both hands at the same time.
Practically, of course, sweeping with
one hand is most common.

60−2

You finish this movement in wider
Shizen Hontai and both hands in
Sotouke Jodan form.

application

Yame
Draw back your right foot into a Shizen Hontai of normal width.
Bring your hands back to the starting position.

Naore
Bring back your left foot and then right foot into Musubidachi.

application of No. 54
Sukuiuke.

NAIFANCHI

Naifanchi kata is historically trained as basic kata among Shurite stylists. Even now together with Pinan katas, Naifanchi is an important basic kata of Shurite type karate.
In short,Naifanchi is a kata to train Naifanchi stance. Naifanchi stance is a basic inner circular stance in which the toes are directed inward. By having the toes inward, you can have your knees a little bit bent inward. And that is very significant from the viewpoint of karate dynamics. The twisting of the body is one of the most important elements of acceleration in karate. So that the twisting of the body works effectively to accelerate techniques, for example punch, the twisting should be made sharply and quickly. Naifanchi stance is ideal for this purpose. If you have your toes outward, you can make a large twisting of the body which takes too much time.
The twisting of the body which takes too long effects your punch negatively. On Naifanchi stance you can make a twist small and sharp which accelerates positively your punch. That is why the beginners generally stand on Naifanchi stance when they perform basic punches.
There are Naifanchi Shodan, Nidan and Sandan. G. Funakoshi has changed the name to Tekki. In some styles this kata is called Tekki Shodan. In Wadoryu Naifanchi Shodan is officially taken up into the training program.
All techniques in this kata should be performed in Jodan instead of Chudan. As you will notice it is more difficult to perform techniques in Jodan than Chudan. It is exactly why the techniques should be performed in Jodan.
Inner circular Naifanchi stance will be further developed to Seishan stance in the following Seishan kata.

Naifanchi stance.

Yoi

Apart from other katas, Naifanchi starts with Heisokudachi (closed toes stance). In Naifanchi stance the toes are directed inward, so it would be proper to have the toes together (which is at least not outward). Place your left hand on your right hand naturally. This posture is called 'Shin no I'.

1-1

1. Make a circle with both hands. Bring back your hands to 'Shin no I' again. Just as in Kushanku kata, the circle gives you a feeling of balance and unification with the universe.

1-2.

1-3.

1-4.

1-5.

1-6.

1-7.

1-6,7. Look to your left first and then your right slowly and calmly.

In budo arts 'Enzan no Metsuke' (en=far, zan = mountain, no = of, me = eyes, tsuke = method) is important. When we perform budo, we should be able to see mountains far away (Enzan). Do not look at a tree alone, but you should have a look over the whole mountain.

Perform this movement slowly and calmly as if you are seeing everything.

2-1. Intermediate

2. Step out with the left and then the right toward your right and have Naifanchi stance.

2-2.

Perform right Tate Shuto (vertical knife-hand) block-punch toward your right. This is a training of taking Naifanchi stance and that of a coordination of side-moving of the body and sideward technique. In Taichi Chuan you can find a similar technique,for example,in 'Single Whip'.

application

3. Perform left Yoko Enpi (sideward elbow strike). Hit your right hand flat as your imaginary target.

Enpi is a short weapon. It is necessary to twist your body sharply, which is the meaning of training here.

4. Twist back your body and have a preparation form. Turn your neck toward the left. We have had similar preparations in Pinan Yodan (No.5 and No. 8) and Pinan Godan (No. 3 and No.6). These are sometimes called 'Horangamae' (egg carrying posture). We generally have it highest in Naifanchi, then Pinan Godan and lowest in Pinan Yodan.

application

6-1. Intermediate

5. Perform left Gedanbarai to your left.

6. Perform right Chokuzuki 45° left, and draw it back immediately and have preparation form.

application

6-2.

7-1. Intermediate

7-1. Step out with the right and then the
left and have Naifanchi stance.

7-2.

8-1. Intermediate

7.2. Perform right Sotouke Jodan at the last minute. Turn your face to the front at the same time.
This kind of stepping (No.2, No.7, and No.23) is sometimes called Chidoriashi (plover step).

8. Perform right Gedanbarai. Take out your left hand once and then draw it back for the momentum acceleration and prepare for the next upward punch.

application

→ next page

8-2.

9-1.

9. Perform left Urazuki (back punch) Jodan.

application

9-2.
Perform left Sotouke Jodan by drawing the hand back from Urazuki.
Have your right hand in Osaeuke (press block) form.

10. Turn your face to the left.

11-1.

11. Sweep with your left foot.
This is a training to check your stance.
Even if you sweep with your foot, you
should keep your balance. This movement also can be used as a block (Nami-
gaeshi) or a sweeping (Ashibarai).

11-2.

Immediately after sweeping, bring
your left foot back and have Naifanchi
stance.

application
avoiding the opponent's sweep

12. Perform left Sotouke Jodan by twisting the upper part of your body. In order to train the twisting of the body, arms should not be moved.

13. Turn your face to the right.

14-1.

14-2.

14. Sweep with your right foot. The same as in No.11. Here the body is twisted to the left, face to the right and sweeping is performed by the right foot.

Bring your right foot back and have Naifanchi stance.

application
blocking the opponent's kick

15. Perform left Uchiuke (inward block) by twisting the upper part of your body. Arms should be kept in the same position. No.12 and No.15 are good training of twisting.

16. Twist back your body to the left and have preparation form. Turn your face to the left at the same time.

application

17. Perform double punch to your left, left straight punch and right Kagizuki (hook punch).

When you perform two punches at the same time, it is very difficult to use the twisting of the body. But still the body must be used to accelerate the punches. In practice, double punches can be used as they are and also, one hand can be used as block and the other as attack.

18. Draw back your hands as if you are trying to get rid of an opponent's seize, by tensing the whole body equally. Tensing is also a good way to learn relaxation. In Nahate karate Sanchin kata is used as basic training where the muscles should be tensed.

application

application

20.

19. Perform right Yoko Enpi by twisting your body. The same as in No.3. Relax a very short while between No.18 and 19.

20-33. The movements are the same as in No. 4 – No.17, but in the opposite direction.

21.

22-1.

22-2.

23-1.

23-2.

24-1.

146 NAIFANCHI

24-2.

25-1.

25-2.

26.

27-1.

27-2.

28.

29.

148 NAIFANCHI

30-1.

30-2.

31.

32.

33.

34.

Yame

Bring back your right foot to have Heisokudachi. Bring back your hands to 'Shin No. I'.

Naore

Open your toes to Musubidachi. Bring your hands to the front of your thigh.

SEISHAN

Seishan kata in Wadoryu comes after Naifanchi kata and before Chinto kata. In Naifanchi kata we have trained different techniques on Naifanchi stance. The purpose of training Naifanchi kata is to learn Naifanchi stance. Naifanchi stance is the most basic of inner circular stances, in which both feet stand on the same line.

Now in Seishan kata we are going to train different techniques on Seishan stances. Seishan stance is also one of the inner circular stances based on the same principle of Naifanchi stance. In Seishan stance the feet are no longer on the same line.
In the first half of Seishan kata Yoko Seishan (sideward Seishan) stance is used with slow and powerful movements. In the latter half Tate Seishan (vertical Seishan) stance is applied with quick movements.
You can see the development of inner circular stances as follows:

Naifanchi — Yoko Seishan — Tate Seishan

The first half should be performed with tension. Tension is a way to learn how to control muscles and yourself. If you can tense and relax your muscles whenever you want, then you are the master of the art. To tense the muscles for the whole time as in the first half of Seishan kata is a way to learn it. This method is often used in Nahate stylists. Nahate stylists regard Sanchin kata as their most important basic kata where they learn the control over the body by tensing.
In Taichi Chuan they try to reach the stage by relaxing the body completely from the beginning to the end.
In Shurite we generally train the combination of relaxation and tension.
Among Shurite stylists Shotokan stylists seem to be tense for a longer period than Wado stylists or Shito stylists.
The purpose of all these different methods is the same: to have a complete control over your body. Look at page 90 for the energy curve.
G. Funakoshi has changed the name of this kata to Hangetsu (han = half, getsu = moon) because of the similarity of inner circular stance to the half moon. Other than this kata, there are various Seishan katas trained in different styles. Nahate stylists have Seisan kata with mostly Sanchin stances. Matsumura no Seishan is closer to Wadoryu Seishan but still it is different. Uechiryu Seishan is also unique, but all these are similar in some respects.

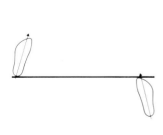

Yoko Seishana stance
(sideward —)

Tate Seishan stance
(vertical —)

1-1.

1-2.

1. From Yoi position (the same way as in Pinan katas) step out with your left foot circularly from the inside and have left Yoko Seishan stance.
Perform left Sotouke Chudan by crossing both hands (left hand under the right). The first half of this kata should be performed slowly and powerfully with tension.

It is necessary to tense the whole body equally. You will find that it is more difficult to make a coordination with slow movements than when you perform them quickly.
In inner circular stances you should always step out circularly. Otherwise, you can not save energy to accelerate the techniques around your hip area.

3-1.

2. Perform right Chokuzuki on the same stance.
In the first half of this kata, techniques should be performed to the lower part. As the center of the body lies about an inch under the navel, it would be proper to perform techniques at around this level to achieve effective tension.
Even Sotouke in No.1 should be performed at a lower level.

3. Step out with your right circurlarly and have right Seishan stance.

3-2.

Perform right Sotouke Chudan.
Try to keep your body straight. Do not
swing your body to the left or to the right
when you step out, otherwise the effect
of circular foot movement disappears.

4. Perform left Chokuzuki.

 →

application

5-1.

5. Step out with your left circularly and have left Seishan stance.

5-2.

Perform left Sotouke Chudan.

application

7-1.

6. Perform right Chokuzuki.

7. Make one-finger-knuckles and draw back your right hand together with your left hand.

7-2.

Perform Hijiuke (elbow block) Jodan with both arms.

8. Thrust out your one-finger knuckles to the lower abdomen. No. 7 (Hijiuke) and No.8 (punch) is a common combination technique.

application

9. Perform Haito (inner knife-hand) Sotouke Jodan with both hands.

10. Perform Shuto (knife-hand) Gedanbarai with both hands. No.6 – No.10 are performed in the same stance. Tense especially your lower abdomen to keep your balance during the performance.

application
Haitouke

application
Shuto Gedanbarai

11-1.

11-2.

11. Turn to the left 180° by moving your right foot toward the left and have left Seishan stance.

Perform right Haito Sotouke Chudan and left Gedanbarai at the same time. Such a double block as this is already trained in Pinan Sandan No.2, No.3, No.5 and No.6. When you want to turn, there are basically two possibilities depending on which foot you move. One is to move the rear foot as we always have done in Pinan katas and Kushanku. The other is to move the front foot as this turning in Seishan kata. The former is better for the training of coordination between turning and technique such as a block. But the latter way is very effective from the viewpoint of avoiding an opponent's attack at the same time as performing a block.

back view

back view

13-1.

12. Perform right Kakeuke (hook block).
Keep your left hand as it is.
Immediately after the Haito Sotouke in
No.11 turn your hand and perform right
Kakeuke.
Haito Sotouke and Kakeuke is a very
common combination. Hooking will be
much easier by combining with Haito
Sotouke.

13. Step out with your right circularly
and have right Seishan stance.

back view

back view

13-2.
Perform left Haito Sotouke Chudan and right Gedanbarai at the same time.

14. Perform left Kakeuke.

back view

back view

15-1.

15. Step out with your left and have left Seishan stance.

15-2.

Perform right Haito Sotouke Chudan and left Gedanbarai at the same time.

application

16. Perform right Kakeuke.

Up to No.16 we have performed techniques slowly and powerfully. From the next movement we are going to perform quickly in normal speed as an application of the stance we have trained in the first half.

17. Turn to the right 90° with Suriashi (gliding) and have right Tate (vertical) Seishan stance.
Perform right Sotouke Jodan.

back view

application

SEISHAN 163

18-1.

18-2.

18. Perform Chokuzuki with your left and right.

application

20-1.

19. Turn to the left 180° with Suriashi (gliding) and have left Tate Seishan stance.
Perform left Sotouke Jodan.

20. Perform Chokuzuki with your right and left.

application

20-2.

21. Turn to the right 90° with Suriashi (gliding) and have right Tate Seishan stance.
Perform right Sotouke Jodan.

side view

22-1.

22. Perform Chokuzuki with your left and right.

22-2.

side view

side view

23-1

23-2

23-1. Raise your left knee and perform
left Uraken (back-fist) upward at the
same time.
Suppose someone attacks you from the
rear; you avoid it by drawing your left
leg forward. At the same time you are
ready to kick an opponent who comes
from the front. Also you perform
Uraken as if you are hitting the opponent's
nose. This is, anyway, a very good training
of balance.

23-2. Turn 180° to the left on your right
foot. Bring down your left foot and perform left Uraken downward Jodan at the
same time.
From No. 23-1 you turn and face the
opponent from the rear. You attack his
leg with your left foot stamping. Perform
Uraken downward to his face by using
downward energy. This is an application
of Pinan Nidan No. 1.

side view

side view

24-1   24-2

24. Step out with your right foot crossing your left. Then perform left Maegeri Chudan and pull your left hand back at the same time.

By stepping out you can reach close to your opponent. (This technique is called Surikomi Maegeri.)

side view

side view

24-3

24-3. Land with your left foot and have left Junzuki Tsukkomi stance.
Perform left Junzuki Tsukkomi Gedan.

25. Pull back your left foot and have left Tate Seishan stance.
Perform right Chokuzuki at the same time.
In No. 24-2 you have given a deep punch in Junzuki Tsukkomi. From there, by twisting your body to the left perform a right punch. A quick change into Seishan stance is the main purpose.

side view

side view

27-1.

26. Perform left Jodanuke.

27—1 Raise your right knee and perform right Uraken upward at the same time. The same as in No. 23-1.

side view

side view

27-2.

27 —2 Turn to the right 180° and perform
right Uraken downward Jodan.
The same as in No. 23-2.

28-1.

28. Step out with your left and then
perform right Maegeri Chudan. Pull back
your right hand.
The same as in No. 24-1.

side view

side view

28-2.

28-3.

28-3. Perform right Junzuki Tsukkomi Gedan.
The same as in No. 24-2.

side view

side view

29. Pull back your right foot and have right Tate Seishan stance.
Perform left Chokuzuki.
The same as in No. 25.

30. Perform right Jodanuke.
The same as in No. 26.

side view

side view

31-1

31-1. Raise up your left knee. Perform Uraken upward with left.
The same as in No. 23-1.

31-2.

31-2. Turn to the left 180° and perform left Uraken downward.
The same as in No. 23-2.

application

application

32-1.

32-1. Perform right Mikazukigeri
(crescent kick) toward your left hand.
Suppose your left hand is being held. You
try to escape by kicking the opponent's
hand with this kick.

32-2.

32-2. Draw back your right foot and have
left Tate Seishan stance.
Perform Chokuzuki with your right.
This combination (drawing back the
kicking foot and perform Gyakuzuki)
is not common though you can see it
even in Ananku kata and Gojushiho kata.

applications

as a block against a punch

as a kick

33-1.

33-1. Draw back your left foot and protect your groin area.
Draw back your hands to prepare for the block.

33-2.

33-2. Perform Shotei Osaeuke (palm-hand press block) with both hands.

application

Yame
Without moving your right foot, bring
your left foot to have Shizen Hontai.

(a)

(b)

(c)

(d)

Application of Seishan stance

The knee can be used to control the
opponent in four different ways.
(a) and (b) are from the outside of the
opponent, (c) and (d) from the inside
of the opponent.

CHINTO

We have started this book with Pinan Shodan and five Pinan katas are summarized into Kushanku kata. Inner circular stance has developed from Naifanchi kata to Seishan kata. These two streams are combined into Chinto kata. Chinto is a light moving kata like Kushanku kata, but it is performed with a stable Seishan stance.

Gichin Funakoshi has changed the name of this kata to Gankaku (gan=rock, kaku=crane), because the posture on one leg in this kata reminds you of a crane standing on a rock.

One leg stance is called Sagiashi (heron stance) and is often seen especially in Tomarite. You can see the same stance in Rohai kata, Wanshu kata, Wankan kata, etc.

Besides this Wadoryu Chinto kata, there is famous Kyan no Chinto (Chinto of Kyan) which is very typical of Tomarite.

Chinto stance

1. Draw back your right foot and have
left Tate Seishan stance.
Perform Jodan Nagashiuke with left over-
hand and right palm-hand on the left side
of your face.
Particularly in this Tate Seishan stance,
have your feet on one line so that you
become smallest against your opponent
from your front. Left hand makes Haishu
Nagashi Sotouke (over-hand, sweep, outward block) and right hand makes Shotei
Nagashi Uchiuke (palm-hand, sweep, in-
dard block). Perform two different blocks
at the same time for training's sake. This
movement is an application of Pinan
Godan No.9. In Nagashiuke you should
perform blocks as if you are sweeping
away the opponent's attack. This is a
basic form of Wadoryu Yakusoku Kumite
(fighting technique training).

2. Perform left Shotei Otoshiuke (palm-
hand downward block) and right Haishu
Otoshiuke (over-hand downward block)
at the same time.
The same movement as in Pinan Godan
No.10 though on a different stance.
Turn your right hand so that it comes
under your left hand. This turning of
hands indicates a Gyakuwaza (seizing the
opponent's hand).
Otoshiuke (downward block) must be
accelerated by the whole body.
Look at page 82 and 83 for
application.

3. Perform left Chokuzuki (straight punch) Chudan.
The same movement as in Pinan Godan No.11. Draw back your right hand sharply to have a stronger punch.

4. Perform right Chokuzuki Chudan.
In order to use the twisting of the body to accelerate the punch, you should open your left foot a little bit so that the stance will be a normal Tate Seishan stance.
The same movement as in Pinan Godan No. 12 though without any stepping out here. The movements from No.1 to No.4 in this kata are the same as in Pinan Godan No.9 to No.12, though the stance is changed to inner circular stance.

5. Turn to the left 360° on your left foot and have Shikoashi stance.
Perform right Gedanbarai.
The same movement as in Pinan Godan No.13.
Suppose your opponent comes from your rear, you draw back your body with the right foot and then you immediately turn to come back to the same place and perform a block against a new attack.

6. Turn to the left 90° and have left Junzuki dachi.
Perform Jujiuke (X-block) Jodan.
The same block as in Pinan Godan No.9 and Kushanku No.57 (though the position of the hands is different).

side view

8-1. Kick with right.

7. Perform Tettsui Otoshiuke (hammer hand downward block) with both hands. The same movement as in Kushanku No.58 (position of the hands is different).

8. Perform Nidangeri (double kick) in the air. Perform Maegeri (front kick) first with right and then left in the air.

8-2.

8-2. Kick with left.

8-3.

8-3. Perform Jujiuke (X-block) Gedan at the moment of landing from the sides of the body into Junzukidachi.

application of jumping

jump and punch

9. Turn 180° to the right on your right foot and have left Junzukidachi. Perform Jujiuke Gedan from the sides of the body. No 8-3 is the back view of this movement.

10. Turn to the right 180° and have Kokutsudachi (back stance). Perform right Gedanbarai while your left hand protects your front part. The Kokutsudachi used here is different from those in Pinan katas, though the weight is on the rear leg about 60%. In this Kokutsudachi, bend your body backward so that you can avoid the opponent's attack to your face, and the front knee is not bent for the purpose of avoiding. This is one of the most important stances in Chinto kata. Look at the last movements of Pinan Godan.
application on page 206.

◄ side view

11-1. Bring your left foot to your right and prepare for the block. Stand up here once so that you can train the avoiding in No. 11-2. This is an intermediate.

11-2. Continue to advance with your left foot and have left Kokutsudachi. Perform left Shuto Gedanbarai. Bring your right Shuto into protection. The same movement as in No.10, though the hands are changed into Shuto. In No.10 and No.11, the body is bent backward to avoid the opponent's attack to the face. At the same time you have a possibility to perform Ashibarai (sweeping with the foot) with your front foot.

side view

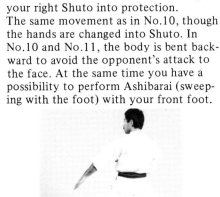

side view

12. Step out with your right and have right Junzukidachi.
Perform Shuto Sotouke Jodan with both hands (right hand inside).

13. Turn to the left 90° and have Hanshiko (half shikoashi — higher than normal shikoashi stance).
Perform Haito Sotouke Jodan with both hands (right hand outside).

side view

side view

14. Stand up slowly into Shizen Hontai (normal natural stance).
Bring down your hands, turning your face to the left. This is a preparation.

15. Step out with your left foot and have left Kokutsudachi.
Perform left Gedanbarai and right Soto-uke Jodan at the same time.
The same movement as in Pinan Godan No.20.

side view

side view

16-1.

16-1. Bring your right foot to your left and stand up once (intermediate).

16-2. Step out further with your right foot and have right Kokutsudachi. Perform left Sotouke Jodan and right Gedanbarai at the same time.
From No.15 to No.17 it is a training of Irimi (entering technique). It is inevitable to stand up once for effective training.

16-2.

side view

side view

17-1.

17-1. Stand up by pulling your left foot.

17-2.

17-2. Continue to turn 360° and step out with your left and have left Kokutsudachi. Perform left Gedanbarai and right Sotouke Jodan.

side view

side view

18-1. Intermediate

18. Bring your right foot to the rear of your left and have left Gyaku-Nekoashi (reverse cat stance).

18-2.

Perform downward Jujiuke from the sides of your body.
Keep your body straight during the performance.

side view

side view

19. Open your right foot and have
Hanshiko (half shikoashi stance).
Perform Sotouke Jodan with both hands.

20. Stand up slowly and have Shizen
Hontai. Bring your hands down.

side view

side view

21. Bring your hands to your hip and prepare for Koteuke (arm block).
The same as in Pinan Sandan No.12 though on a different stance.

22. Lower your body and twist to the left.
Perform right Koteuke.
The same kind of block as in Pinan Sandan No.13.

side view

side view

23. Twist back your body to the right.
Perform left Koteuke.

24. Turn 180° to the right on your right
foot and have right Gyaku Nekoashi
stance.
Perform Sotouke Jodan with both hands.

side view

side view

194 CHINTO

25-1. The following three movements should be performed at the same time. Raise your left knee up as if you are ready to kick.
Right Sotouke Jodan.
Left Gedanbarai.

25-2. Bring your hands back as in Pinan Yodan No.5, left hand on your right hand. Keep standing on Sagiashi stance.

side view

side view

25-3. Perform left Gedanbarai and left Maegeri at the same time.
The same movement as in Pinan Yodan No.6.

25-4. Step out with your right and perform right Junzuki.

No. 25 is very characteristic of Chinto kata. Suppose your opponent sweeps you with his Bo (stick) or his foot. You avoid it by raising your left foot. Then his attack comes to your Chudan, so you block with left Gedanbarai and counter-attack with your left kick, which is followed by your right Junzuki.
This will give you an excellent training of quickness and balance.

side view ➞

26-1. Draw back your right foot and have left Sagiashidachi.
Perform left Sotouke Jodan and right Gedanbarai at the same time.

26-2. Prepare your right hand on your left hand as in Pinan Yodan No.8.

side view

side view

26-3. Perform right Gedanbarai and right Maegeri at the same time.

26-4. Perform left Gyakuzuki on right Tate Seishan stance.

side view

side view

27-1. Turn to the left 180° and raise your left leg.
Perform right Sotouke Jodan and left Gedanbarai at the same time.
The same movement as in No.25-1.

27-2. Bring your left hand to your right hand. The same movement as in No.25-2.

side view

side view

27-3. Perform left Gedanbarai and left Maegeri at the same time.
The same movement as in No.25-3.

27-4. Perform right Gyakuzuki on left Tate Seishan stance.

side view

side view

28. Turn to the right 180° and have Shikoashi stance.
Perform right Kakeuke (hook block) Jodan. application on page 207.

29. Perform left Tate Enpi (vertical elbow strike).
The stance is changed to right Tate Seishan stance. The body twisting must be used to accelerate the Enpi.

side view

side view

30. Twist your body back a little bit and draw back your left hand to the side of your body in Shotei (palm-hand) form and right fist in front of your left hand. This is a preparation for the next movement and at the same time this indicates a Gyakuwaza (seizing the opponent's hand). Application on page 207.

31-1. Turn to the right 180° on your right Sagishi stance.
Perform right Ipponken (one-finger punch) to the opponent's nose by using the turning of the body.
No.30 and No.31 can be used in Gyakuwaza.
Application on page 207.

side view

side view

31-2.

31-3.
31-3. Prepare your left hand on your right.
The same movement as in No.25-2.

side view

side view

31-4. Perform left Gedanbarai and left Maegeri at the same time.
The same movement as in No. 25-3.

31-5. Step out with your right and perform right Junzuki.
The same movement as in No. 25-4.

side view

side view

Yame
Turn to the left 180° by drawing your
left foot and have Shizen hontai.

Application of No.10, 11 of Chinto.
Avoiding the opponent's punch to your face by bending the body back or by using your right hand, hook his front foot with your right.

Continue with your counterpunch.

application of No.28.

application of No.30 — (1)

application of No.30 —(2).

KICKS IN KATAS

There are various kinds of kicks in karate, but the kicks used in katas are mostly Maegeri (front kick). Generally speaking, the kicks are performed by using the movement of bending — stretching of the knee. Various combinations of the movements of the knee joint and the hip joint make various kicks.

Kingeri . . . . .bend knee — lift thigh forward — stretch knee
(groin kick)   (using instep as weapon)

Maegeri . . . . .bend knee — lift thigh forward — stretch knee
(front kick)   (using ball of the foot as weapon)

Yokogeri . . . . . . .bend knee — lift thigh forward — stretch knee
(side kick)   and open sideward

Ushirogeri . . . . . .bend knee — lift thigh forward — stretch knee
(back kick)   and swing backward

Mawashigeri . . . . .bend knee — lift thigh sideward — stretch knee
(round kick)   and swing forward

Therefore the most important thing is to train the movement of bending and stretching of the knee. Maegeri is probably enough to represent most of the kicking techniques.